Lerner SPORTS

SPORTS
ALL-ST★RS

SUE BIRD

Christina Hill

Lerner Publications ◆ Minneapolis

SPORTS THRILLS
MEET
RESEARCH SKILLS

Lerner SPORTS

Free Database Trial: **lernersports.com**

Lerner Publications Company
An imprint of Lerner Publishing Group, Inc.
241 First Avenue North
Minneapolis, MN 55401 USA

For reading levels and more information, look up this title at www.lernerbooks.com.

Main body text set in Albany Std. Typeface provided by Agfa.

Library of Congress Cataloging-in-Publication Data

Names: Hill, Christina, author.
Title: Sue Bird / Christina Hill.
Description: Minneapolis : Lerner Publications , [2022] | Series: Sports all-stars (lerner sports) | Includes bibliographical references and index. | Summary: "Four-time WNBA champion Sue Bird of the Seattle Storm is a basketball legend. She is also a vocal social-justice advocate and a community leader. Read about her life and career on and off the court"— Provided by publisher.
Identifiers: LCCN 2021022650 (print) | LCCN 2021022651 (ebook) | ISBN 9781728441177 (library binding) | ISBN 9781728449401 (paperback) | ISBN 9781728445137 (ebook)
Subjects: LCSH: Bird, Sue. | Women basketball players—United States—Biography—Juvenile literature.
Classification: LCC GV884.B572 H55 2022 (print) | LCC GV884.B572 (ebook) | DDC 796.323092 [B]—dc23

LC record available at https://lccn.loc.gov/2021022650
LC ebook record available at https://lccn.loc.gov/2021022651

Manufactured in the United States of America
1-49888-49731-7/15/2021

TABLE OF CONTENTS

FIERCE COMEBACK

Sue Bird dribbles the ball in 2018.

Game 5 of the Women's National Basketball Association (WNBA) Semifinals took place on September 4, 2018. Sue Bird and the Seattle Storm were up against the Phoenix Mercury. The game marked the end of the season for one team. With only five minutes left, Seattle trailed by four points. They needed to turn the game around to stay alive in the playoffs.

- **Date of birth:**
  October 16, 1980

- **Position:** point guard

- **League:** WNBA

- **Professional highlights:**
  three-time WNBA champion;
  all-time WNBA leader in games
  played; four-time Olympic
  gold-medal winner

- **Personal highlights:** grew up
  in Syosset, New York; played
  soccer and ran track in high
  school; engaged to soccer
  superstar Megan Rapinoe

Bird wears a face guard to protect her broken nose.

Bird decided to make this game unforgettable. She had broken her nose in Game 4 and stopped playing to receive treatment. The Storm lost. Armed with a face mask to protect her nose in Game 5, Bird focused on only one thing. She wanted to win. The last five minutes of Game 5 might be the best of Bird's incredible career.

Bird soared across the court to score 14 points in five minutes. The Storm won 94–84. "As far as stretches go, it's up there," Bird said. "I don't know if I've had a fourth quarter like that in such a big game in my life." And the rest of the world agreed. Fellow basketball players Kobe Bryant and LeBron James took to social media to applaud Bird's impressive clutch performance.

Bird keeps the ball away from a defender during a college game.

Suzanne Brigit Bird was born on October 16, 1980. She grew up in Syosset, New York. Sue played soccer and ran track. Her older sister, Jennifer,

Bird (*center*) and some of her college
teammates celebrate a big win.

played basketball. Sue wanted to be just like her. Sue
had a competitive nature and always wanted to win. Her
natural talent emerged when she started playing Amateur
Athletic Union basketball in elementary school.

Sue played basketball at Christ the King Regional High
School in Queens, New York. The school had a good
team. With Sue's help, Christ the King won every game
they played in her senior year. They even won the New
York state championship in 1997 and 1998.

Sue played point guard, an important position on the court. Point guards are responsible for the team's offense. They have to protect the ball and pass it to the right players.

"It has to be team play," Sue said. "You make the extra pass, do the little things. I know I'm not the biggest or the quickest. But with my brain I can make a difference."

Colleges were impressed by Sue's skill. Many schools wanted her to play on their teams. She chose the University of Connecticut (UConn). UConn is known for having an excellent women's basketball team. And in Connecticut, Sue wouldn't be far from home and her family.

Bird cheers after winning an important game with the UConn Huskies.

Unfortunately, Bird had a knee injury during her freshman year at UConn. But she fought hard to recover and come back. She was a key player on the team. The Huskies went on to win the 2000 and 2002 Women's College Basketball National Championships.

Bird set her goals even higher. She was on a mission to play in the WNBA. She had worked hard to prove she was ready.

The New York Knicks were Bird's favorite team to watch when she was a kid.

Bird helped UConn defeat Oklahoma in the Women's College Basketball National Championship game in 2002.

At the WNBA Draft, teams take turns choosing new players. Being the first pick on draft day means that WNBA officials consider that athlete to be the best player available. In 2002, Bird was the first pick in the WNBA Draft. The Storm chose her, and she's been one of the league's best players ever since.

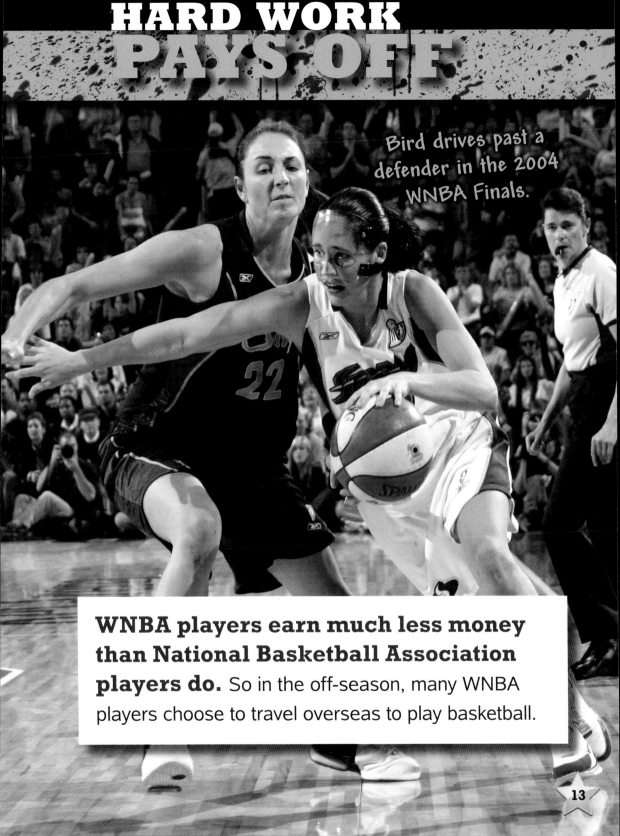

Bird drives past a defender in the 2004 WNBA Finals.

WNBA players earn much less money than National Basketball Association players do. So in the off-season, many WNBA players choose to travel overseas to play basketball.

Bird played pro basketball in Russia during the WNBA off-season.

Bird played in the Russian Premier League, where she made four times her WNBA salary. She played in Russia on three different teams from 2004–2007 and 2011–2014.

Traveling overseas to play basketball is challenging. Players often feel homesick. Playing during the WNBA off-season leaves athletes with little time for rest

Even when she played in Russia, Bird always wore a number 10 jersey.

or vacation. Bird fights for female players to earn more money in the US so they don't have to play overseas.

Bird's time in Russia taught her to take care of her own health and exercise routines. She said, "When you're overseas, you're truly on your own."

Bird led the Storm to the WNBA playoffs for the first time in team history during her first season.

When Bird joined the WNBA in 2002, the league was just five years old. She didn't have many older players to look up to. Now with almost 20 years of pro basketball experience, Bird gives advice to new players. She tells young athletes that it is never too early to start caring about their health and nutrition. Many athletes retire from basketball in their mid-30s. But Bird has no plans to quit as she glides into her 40s in great shape.

Bird follows the 80/20 diet. She eats healthful foods about 80 percent of the time. She saves less-healthful treats for the remaining 20 percent. Her favorite meals are brown rice bowls, sweet potatoes, vegetables, and chicken.

Yoga and stretching have helped Bird's body recover from injuries. She trains hard but likes to mix it up so she doesn't get bored. Bird loves to swim, lift weights, and ride her bike. On game days, she has an hour-long practice with her team before heading home for a power nap. The extra rest gives her body a boost of energy before the big game.

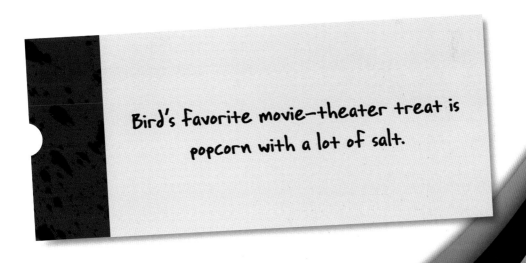

Bird's favorite movie—theater treat is popcorn with a lot of salt.

Bird with her girlfriend,
Megan Rapinoe

Bird is a five-time Olympic gold-medal winner.

On October 30, 2020, Bird and Megan Rapinoe announced they were getting married. The couple met at the 2016 Olympic Games in Rio de Janeiro, Brazil. Rapinoe is one of the world's best soccer players. Together, the couple fights for social

WNBA players Stefanie Dolson (left), Devereaux Peters (center), and Bird played ping-pong at the 8th annual TopSpin New York charity event.

justice and supports the Black Lives Matter movement. Black Lives Matter works to end violence against Black people. Bird and Rapinoe also work hard to expand the opportunities available to female athletes.

Bird loves to give back to her community and supports youth programs like the Boys & Girls Clubs of America.

She led a group of 45 girls at StormAcademy, a special educational session in Seattle, Washington. Bird taught the girls leadership and team-building skills.

Z Girls is another charity group that is important to Bird. Z Girls helps empower young female athletes and build their confidence to play sports. Bird has earned many awards recognizing her charity work.

Bird is not a fan of ocean swimming. Sharks and seaweed scare her.

Bird and Rapinoe are two of the most famous faces in women's sports.

In 2019, the disease COVID-19 began spreading. The pandemic affected the entire world. In 2020, stay-at-home orders in the US kept many people at home, including athletes. With the WNBA schedule disrupted, Bird found ways to keep busy. She and Rapinoe hosted *A Touch More*, an Instagram Live show with special celebrity guests and fun activities to do at home. Fans could join the show on Instagram Live and ask questions, send comments, and see how Bird and Rapinoe live off the court.

Bird spent many summers selling ice cream.

Bird shows off her fourth WNBA Championship trophy after the Storm defeated the Las Vegas Aces in 2020.

Bird is certain to join the Women's Basketball Hall of Fame someday.

But retirement is not on her mind. Bird has spent her entire WNBA career with the Storm and plans to continue playing with them. In 2020, Bird helped her team win their fourth WNBA championship.

The Storm is one of only three WNBA teams to win four league championships.

Bird is the WNBA's all-time career leader with 2,972 assists. She ranks eighth in career points with 6,422. And she is the leader in games started and minutes played. She has been in 11 WNBA All-Star Games and has more playoff appearances than any other player.

Bird dribbles the ball up the court for the USA Basketball Women's National Team in 2020.

Bird has also represented the US at the Olympics and other international events. "For us there wasn't a WNBA growing up," Bird said. "The Olympics was the end all, be all for what a women's basketball player could do. You could go to college, to the Final Four, then the Olympics and that was really it. To achieve it one time was like a dream come true." But Bird achieved that dream five times. In 2021, Bird and the USA Basketball Women's National Team won gold at the Olympics in Tokyo, Japan. It was Bird's fifth gold medal, and the seventh straight gold medal for the team.

Bird celebrated her 40th birthday in 2020. She is one of the oldest WNBA players. But Bird wants to keep playing. And she will never truly leave basketball behind her. It is certain that Bird will continue to be a success both on and off the court.

All-Star Stats

Scoring points is important, but basketball is a team sport. Looking at how many assists a player earns is a key factor for an amazing all-around player. Take a look at where Bird ranks in career assists in the **WNBA**.

WNBA Career Leaders for Assists

1.	Sue Bird	2,888
2.	Ticha Penicheiro	2,600
3.	Lindsay Whalen	2,345
4.	Courtney Vandersloot	2,022
5.	Diana Taurasi	1,953
6.	Becky Hammon	1,708
7.	Cappie Pondexter	1,578
8.	Tamika Catchings	1,488
9.	Shannon Johnson	1,424
10.	Tanisha Wright	1,422

Glossary

assist: a pass from a teammate that leads directly to a score

charity: aid given to those in need

clutch: a tight or critical situation

competitive: wanting to win or be the best at something

draft: when teams take turns choosing new players

drill: a physical activity done repeatedly to learn a skill

pandemic: occurring over a wide area and usually affecting a large number of people

point guard: the player who leads a basketball team on offense

semifinal: a game or a series of games coming before the final round in a tournament

yoga: a system of body positions and breathing methods that help physical and emotional well-being

7   Matt Calkins, "One for the Ages: Storm Gets Crown Jewel in Classic WNBA Semifinals Victory over Phoenix," *Seattle Times*, September 4, 2018, https://www .seattletimes.com/sports/storm/one-for-the-ages-storm -gets-crown-jewel-in-classic-wnba-victory-over-phoenix/.

10 Filip Bondy, "Sue Bird, U.S. Women's Olympic Basketball Team Ready to Fly," *Daily News*, August 8, 2008, https ://www.nydailynews.com/sports/sue-bird-u-s-women -olympic-basketball-team-ready-fly-article-1.315632.

15 Christopher Cason, "The Real-Life Diet of Sue Bird, Basketball Legend," *GQ*, June 11, 2018, https://www .gq.com/story/real-life-diet-sue-bird.

23 Collette Reitz. "WNBA Superstar Sue Bird Works Hard, Plays Hard, & Takes Nothing for Granted," *Elite Daily*, April 13, 2020, https://www.elitedaily.com/p/wnba- superstar-sue-bird-works-hard-plays-hard-takes-nothing- for-granted-22798742.

26 Jeff Metcalfe, "Diana Taurasi, Sue Bird Peek Toward What Could Be Their Fifth Olympics," *Arizona Republic*, March 30, 2021, https://www.azcentral.com/story/sports /wnba/mercury/2021/03/30/diana-taurasi-sue-bird-look -toward-what-could-their-fifth-olympics/4806970001/.

Learn More

Buckey, A. W. *Women in Basketball*. Lake Elmo, MN: Focus Readers, 2020.

Labrecque, Ellen. *WNBA Champions*. Mankato, MN: The Child's World, 2020.

Scheff, Matt. *NBA and WNBA Finals*. Minneapolis: Lerner Publications, 2021.

Seattle Storm
https://storm.wnba.com

USA Basketball
https://www.usab.com

WNBA
https://www.wnba.com

Index

Photo Acknowledgments

Rob Carr/Staff/Getty Images, p.4; Rob Carr/Staff/Getty Images, p.6; Andy Lyons/Staff/Getty Images, p.8; UPI Photo Service/Newscom, p.9; Andy Lyons/Staff/Getty Images, p.10; Andy Lyons/Staff/Getty Images, p.12; Otto Greule Jr/Stringer/Getty Images, p.13; Dmitry Argunov/Alamy, p.14; Dmitry Golubovich/ZUMA Press/Newscom, p.15; KARL CRUTCHFIELD, Ai Wire / "Ai Wire Photo Service/Newscom, p.16; Ethan Miller/Staff/Getty Images, p.18; Tom Pennington/Staff/Getty Images, p.19; Ben Gabbe/Stringer/Getty Images, p.20; Ezra Shaw/Staff/Getty Images, p.22; Romanova Anna/Shutterstock, p.23; Julio Aguilar/Stringer/Getty Images, p.24; Julio Aguilar/Stringer/Getty Images, p.25; Joe Robbins/Stringer/Getty Images, p.26

Cover: Christian Petersen/Staff/Getty Images